When Your Child Says "I Do"

Letting Go and Loving Well

Chris Polski

New Growth Press
newgrowthpress.com

New Growth Press, Greensboro, NC 27401
newgrowthpress.com

Cover Design: Dan Stelzer
Interior Typesetting and Ebook: Lisa Parnell

ISBN: 978-1-64507-617-9 (paperback)
ISBN: 978-1-64507-618-6 (ebook)

Library of Congress Cataloging-in-Publication Data on file

Printed in India

30 29 28 27 26 1 2 3 4 5

Therefore, a man shall leave his father and his mother and hold fast to his wife, and they shall become one flesh.
—Genesis 2:24

As the wedding sparklers fizzled out into the night air, we watched as our daughter and her husband drove away to their new life together. Just as their taillights were fading in the distance, my wife turned to me and asked the very question I was thinking: "Are they going to be okay?"

In the wake of such a joyful celebration, a brooding sense of uncertainty lingered. We were no longer the main people in our daughter's world. Just as Scripture describes, she was now responsible for building her life together with her husband—our new son.

While excitement filled our hearts for their next chapter, we found ourselves wondering, *What do our roles look like now that our child is embarking on this new adventure? What should we do, and what should we definitely not do?*

Learning to be good parents to newlyweds was beginning to feel overwhelming. It was as if we needed premarital counseling all over again—but this time, for us as parents.

What we were experiencing was the parental side of leaving and cleaving, a little-talked-about process that is just as mysterious and challenging for parents as it is for the new bride and groom.

This minibook is designed to help parents who are navigating this transition to better understand what it means to *let go* and *love well.* None of us will do this perfectly. We certainly haven't. But making a prayerful effort can make a significant difference in your life and the life of your child and their new spouse.

Biblical and Practical Insights on Parenting Newly Married Adult Children

In the adjustment to becoming parents of newlyweds, you may have been tempted to look for strategies to change the way your child and new son- or daughter-in-law relate to you. However, this usually proves difficult because we cannot change others. What we can do, with the Holy Spirit's help, is work on ourselves and approach this time of transition with grace and biblical wisdom.

The new couple's responsibility

It is helpful to begin with a few reminders about the biblical expectations for new couples to leave, cleave, and "become one flesh" (Genesis 2:24). Understanding what this means for our children can help us reframe our own role as they enter marriage.

To *leave* means to redefine one's understanding of home. A newly married couple must form a household with its own values and its own unique culture. While families of origin remain important, they can no longer be the central reference point for a newlywed. A humorous but illustrative reminder of this is the classic wedding anecdote about the new wife who finds herself in her first big fight with her husband. In desperation, she calls her parents wanting to "go home." Her parents immediately and wisely respond, "Honey, you *are* home!"

To *cleave* (or "hold fast") is a term often used to describe the covenantal bond between God and his people. It refers to the process of bonding deeply to something by forming a new unity without losing one's individual identity. This union redefines how the two people inside of it must now navigate the world: *together*. Think of riders on a tandem bike. Both maintain their distinct roles, but they must work together in harmony lest the bike tumble over.

Becoming one flesh involves more than establishing physical intimacy—it signifies a comprehensive expectation that two people will merge their lives together. It's such a complete union that in Ephesians 5, Paul describes this process as a "mystery" that reflects the spiritual relationship between Christ and the church (v. 32). Such a union requires the couple to work continually at the co-creation of a shared life perspective. Even mundane decisions, like scheduling an outing with friends, now require a degree of mutual consideration.

This biblical call to leave, cleave, and "become one flesh" rests squarely on the shoulders of the new couple, and it is important for them to heed this call as they build their new life together.

The parents' experience

Even though it is biblical for a new couple to create a new home together, this transition can be both confusing and painful for parents as it involves loss. We parents are being left, *un-cleaved* from, and *separated* from our own flesh.

It's just as we begin to experience this sense of loss that we need to lean into what Scripture teaches us about our ultimate role in our children's lives. Proverbs 22:6 lays it out concisely when it tells us to "train up a child in the way he should go."

Training up a child refers to the process of guiding them along the narrow path of life, gently correcting them when they stray and cheering them on when they succeed. But notice that there is also a goal for the child: The child must *go*. They must follow their path, wherever the Lord leads—and we must let them. Even more—and I know this is hard—we must *want* them to. If God has led them into marriage, then leaving us and becoming one with their spouse is the path they must follow—and we must support them in that path.

Several years ago, my wife and I were socializing with a woman whose daughter had recently married and then quickly moved out of town. This mother was devastated. She advised that before we let our children marry, we should first get assurance that they would not relocate to a distant location. If they didn't agree, her counsel was that we should refuse to bless the marriage.

While her heart to remain near to her child was understandable, she was missing this most essential aspect of our role in parenting: to prepare our children to follow *God's* path for their lives, not *our* path.

As our adult children begin the process of leaving and cleaving, they will naturally (and rightly) begin to shift their primary allegiance from us to their spouse. This means that we parents are going to move down their priority list. It's essential to recognize that this doesn't mean that they love us any less. Instead, this shows that they have rightly prioritized their marriage—and eventually their own children—more than our wishes, wants, and desires.

As our child leaves us, cleaves to their spouse, and becomes one flesh with them, we naturally feel a sense of loss. We feel like we have been separated from our own flesh. We might compare this feeling to what it might be like to donate a kidney. A kidney donor gives something essential away. The organ that once belonged to her now belongs to another and is just as essential to that person's current thriving as it once was to hers.

There's no way around it. The process of letting our newly married children go is a major challenge, though not one that is insurmountable with the Lord's help.

Rethinking parenting styles for adult children

Another important factor that parents need to consider is how to adjust their parenting style—their manner of engagement and expectation—with their adult children.

In her extensive research, clinical psychologist Diana Baumrind identified four overarching parenting styles using the two measures of *involvement* (the degree of parental engagement in the child's life) and *expectation* (the degree to which a child is expected to conform to a parent's belief system). Although these categories were written to describe the parent/child relationship before adulthood, these descriptions are also helpful for evaluating the parent/adult child dynamic:

1. Authoritative (high involvement, high expectation)
2. Authoritarian (low involvement, high expectation)
3. Permissive (high involvement, low expectation)
4. Neglectful (low involvement, low expectation)[1]

Authoritative parenting—high expectations with high emotional engagement—is ideal for the season when our children are still at home and under our authority. But this style of parenting is far less suitable once our children reach full adulthood or marry, because at that point, they are no longer called to obey us. Instead, the best approach for parenting married adult children leans toward permissive—high parental involvement with low expectations. In this context, *permissive* doesn't refer to accepting moral laxity; it simply means staying relationally close to our children without placing too much pressure on them to conform to our expectations. In other words, be available, not overbearing. Offer help, not control.

This can be highly disconcerting for most parents who have spent their whole lives trying to walk the fine line of maintaining a meaningful relationship with their child while also enforcing basic rules and regulations that will help them mature into adulthood. It can also be complicated by an adult child's poor decision-making or ungodly behavior. In this latter scenario, a parent can still lovingly assert their biblical convictions but should work just as hard at maintaining open channels of communication.

From here, I'd like to offer three practical strategies that we can employ in the early stages of our children's married lives in our ongoing effort to let go and love well, followed by one final reflection on how to respond when we find ourselves in conflict with our newly married adult children.

Practical Strategies for Letting Go and Loving Well

There's nothing like seeing your new father-in-law in his underwear.

That was my thought years ago on our first family beach trip with my wife's family, crammed into a condo with three generations and two bathrooms. I was patiently waiting my turn for the bathroom when my father-in-law called out that it was clear. I assumed that he had already stepped out as I rounded the corner, but I was wrong. He was just then exiting while still wearing nothing but his tighty-whities. I averted my eyes, embarrassed, but he walked by casually and said, "Welp, you're in the family now."

While I'd received their blessing to marry their daughter and been given their affirmations that they loved me, that awkward encounter, as strange as it may seem, was what made me feel like I was fully part of the family.

My experience being blended into my wife's family went smoothly, but many parents struggle to connect with their new child-in-law. This struggle usually emerges as we sort through contrasting styles of expectation between our family and that of our new child-in-law, our own insecurities about our bond with our child, or experiences in which deep family loyalties may be put to the test. These difficulties can be further exacerbated when the new child-in-law comes from a different ethnic or cultural context than our own. Even though such challenges exist, there are ways to proactively address them.

1. Make it clear that your new child-in-law is your child

The book of Ruth illustrates beautifully how parents-in-law can communicate that their child-in-law is truly one of the family. Ruth, a young widow, famously chooses to stay with her mother-in-law, Naomi, saying, "Your people shall be my people, and your God my God" (Ruth 1:16). But notice that just before this Naomi had already declared that Ruth and Orpah were her "daughters" (Ruth 1:11). Naomi, despite deep personal loss, receives Ruth as her true daughter. They walk together through grief and renewal for the rest of their days. As parents-in-law, we can embody Naomi's heart through small but meaningful actions.

For example, it's easy to fall into the habit of constantly introducing your child's new spouse as your son- or daughter-in-law. This is understandable and often helps to avoid confusion. But consider changing things up from time to time by referring to your new child-in-law as your "son" or "daughter," especially in direct conversation. Doing this sends a signal that they are a full part of the family.

And just as you would with your own child, let them see the unfiltered version of your family as often as you can, whether it's being open about struggles you might be facing or simply not tidying up the house for every visit. This kind of authenticity builds trust and communicates to your child's spouse that they are on the inside. For example, in the early days of our marriage, my father-in-law was facing a daunting cancer diagnosis. Gradually, as we got to know each other better, he began to share more with me about the struggle he was going through, helping me feel more deeply connected to my wife's family.

Work to establish an independent relationship with them as they find their footing as your new child. My son-in-law loves soccer and collecting vinyl records. I relate very well to the first, and not so well to the second. So every once in a while, I try to slip a question into the conversation about what new records he's come across. Ask your child-in-law about their passions and look for ways to connect with them beyond the existing connections with your own child.

If they live close by, bring them along for outings and everyday activities like fishing trips, shopping days, or movie nights. One friend of mine built strong bonds with his three sons-in-law by intentionally spending time hunting, golfing, or working on home improvement projects with them. Over time, his sons-in-law have grown into seeing one another as brothers while also feeling more and more like sons to my friend and his wife, thus strengthening the overall bonds in their family.

Most importantly, pray for your child-in-law *individually* in addition to praying for them as a couple. Ask what they need prayer for or simply pray a passage of Scripture for them, like Ephesians 3:14–19, which lays out some beautiful spiritual pursuits for anyone's life.

The question of what your child's spouse calls you can be a tricky topic that I've found most easily navigated by opening the conversation with your biological child first. Ask her if she and her husband have talked about it, and if they haven't, offer some suggestions you would be comfortable with. If your child-in-law has already begun to refer to you as "Mom" or "Dad," while it may be uncomfortable for you, try to give them the benefit of the doubt that they are probably doing it to honor you.

These intentional actions will communicate that you love not just your own child, but their spouse, whom you see as your child too. And that is a blessing every son- or daughter-in-law needs to receive.

2. Give them space to sort out their own family rhythms and traditions

"All right, everybody! It's time for the annual 'Invent Your Own Sandwich' Night!"

This quirky post-Thanksgiving tradition marked a highlight in one family's annual holiday celebrations. Using leftovers and odd ingredients, everyone invented their own unique sandwich—no help allowed. Initially, most of the children's concoctions were inedible. But as they grew, so did their creativity. This goofy competition eventually turned into a cherished family event, complete with a homemade mayonnaise-jar trophy awarded to the winner. Even as the children left for college, they made it a point to return home for this unique Thanksgiving tradition.

Eventually, the oldest son married and relocated. When he and his new wife called to say that they wouldn't be able to make it to Thanksgiving, the parents were very disappointed and asked if he might just come alone. When he hesitated, one parent half-joked, "Well, I guess this is how the tradition finally ends." That off-handed comment landed harshly, causing the son to feel guilty and his wife to feel that she caused the end of the tradition that the parents so valued.

Moments like these are common when children marry and family traditions clash with emerging realities. As parents, we naturally invest in traditions that connect our families. However, we must learn along the way to hold them loosely so that we can preserve what matters most: the relationship.

We need to give our newly married children space to decide which traditions of ours they want to keep, which might need to be adjusted, and which might have to be discontinued so that they can create traditions of their own.

Here are a few guiding principles that can help you in your efforts to give your newly married children space.

- *Remember the early days of your own marriage.* When tensions rise around traditions and holidays, recall what it felt like navigating your own parents' and in-laws' expectations when you were a newlywed. Chances are, you'll remember the guilt, the frustration, and the struggle to please everyone that may have been a part of your own story. Even if you had relatively few issues, don't assume that this is going to be your children's experience. Those memories, whatever they are, should help you to foster greater empathy and patience toward your own children.
- *Keep the main thing the main thing.* It's easy to become attached to the traditions we've created, whether it's holding a sandwich competition or always going to the same restaurant for a birthday celebration. But remember, the ultimate goal isn't keeping the tradition going; *the ultimate goal is maintaining connection with our kids.* That means that if Thanksgiving needs to

shift to another house or the birthday dinner to a different restaurant, the joy of being together can remain.

- *Let them initiate.* Early in their marriage, give your children space to lead the planning. If they don't want to initiate, find an appropriate moment to casually ask, "Hey, have you guys thought about Thanksgiving yet? We're flexible—just let us know." They may have ideas they're hesitant to share because they don't follow the existing traditions in your family. Be open to different ideas and invest in long-term relational development.

But what if your child and son or daughter-in-law don't ever want to spend time with you? Of course, this is a nagging fear for many parents. If your child and their spouse consistently avoid spending time in your company, it could be a sign of a serious problem that should be addressed with the help of a pastor or a counselor.

Even if there aren't deep-seated problems, some couples may not wish to participate in family events as often as their parents would like them to. Situations like these are precisely when our faith in Christ must guide us. Ephesians 4:1–3 urges us to approach relationships with humility, gentleness, patience, and love. Forbearance, which anticipates the need to offer grace, is key. When we face disappointments, our identity in Christ should shape our responses more than our identity as parents.

3. Model for them how marital love can mature over time

There's a popular saying: *Getting married is easy; staying married is hard.* Unfortunately, most of us don't fully understand that until we've lived it. This is because the person you married isn't the same person you are married to today. And that's a good thing. Tim Keller wrote, "When you get married, you and your spouse are a couple of 'change-ists.' You're going to change, and so is your spouse."[2] Let your child and new son- or daughter-in-law see how this truth has played out in your relationship—especially in humorous, relatable ways.

Early in our marriage, my wife and I had our fair share of arguments. One night we had a major argument. Eventually, after I had angrily left the room, she stuffed my jacket into a greasy pizza box on the kitchen counter and tossed it in the garage trash can, knowing I'd find it while looking for my jacket or taking out the trash in the morning.[3]

By God's grace, we both repented the next day. While we laugh about it now, it's a reminder of how far we've come. Sadly, many couples don't make it through these early trials. Statistics show that around 40–45 percent of first marriages end in divorce, most within the first seven years.[4]

As parents, you have a unique opportunity to show your children that lasting love and a deepening sense of partnership are possible. Be open about your own journey. Let them see that bumps in the road are normal, and that ups and downs are a critical part of the process of developing a thriving marriage. If you are divorced or have experienced the death of a spouse, you have an equally important opportunity to share your story with your adult children.

My parents, now married nearly forty years, respond to conflict with humor and grace. Early on in their marriage, however, the same kind of conflict might have caused major arguments. What I've observed over time is that their love has matured, and that gives my wife and me continued hope for our own future.

In addition to reminding them that marital love grows and matures over time, here are some important ways to encourage your newly married child and child-in-law:

- *Remind them that hard times will come and go.* Jesus said, "In the world you will have tribulation. But take heart; I have overcome the world" (John 16:33). So share your stories about the trouble you've encountered in this world, right alongside the stories of how God has delivered you. This will help them keep perspective when they face their own difficulties.
- *Encourage them to prioritize their marriage.* As life gets busy, especially as children come along, it's easy for young couples to lose connection. If you've learned this the hard way, share your lessons. Support your newly married children by making it possible in little

ways (e.g., targeted financial gifts, pet-sitting, and eventually babysitting) for them to carve out meaningful time with each other as often as they can.

- *Point them to wise but independent counsel.* If talking directly with your children about these things has been awkward, encourage them to find older mentors. A number of couples in our church have been married for over fifty years. They all still share doting smiles, playful kisses, and affectionate needling of one another. I love to encourage younger couples in our church to spend time with one of these couples, asking them what they've learned along the way. They will be the first to tell you that their journeys weren't easy—but they were worth it.
- *Remember to listen.* Although your personal experiences may provide wisdom for a young couple, it is important to exercise discernment in when and how you share. For example, it may not be wise to jump into your own stories right away, especially when a child may first need to open up about what they are going through. Instead, take time to ask them clarifying questions about what's going on in their lives. Make sure they feel heard before you begin to talk. And if they do ask for advice, share it humbly by recognizing that each marriage is unique. Let them draw their own

conclusions from your experiences, and avoid stating any moral imperatives for their marriage based only on your own experience.

What If My Children Aren't Responding?

The Bible is clear that when our children leave our home, and especially when they marry, they no longer owe us obedience, only honor (Deuteronomy 5:16; Ephesians 6:1–4). Understanding why our adult children may not be responding to us in what we consider an honorable way requires us to reflect honestly on two foundational questions: First, are we making sure that we are assessing the difficult situation based on the concept of honor and not obedience? Second, are we confident that some current or past aspect of our own sin and brokenness isn't at the root of the problem?

Understanding honor

The biblical word for honor comes from a root that means something like *heavy*, in the sense that something or someone is significant or worthy.[5] To honor someone is to act in such a way that we recognize their significance and treat them accordingly.

Parents of newly married children feel the most temptation toward anger when our children don't see things the way we do. This is because we know very well just how significant we were in nurturing their life for all those years that they were in our home. None of us were perfect, but we made sacrifices, we exercised great forgiveness, and we were generous. We loved our child even when our child didn't demonstrate the same love in return.

But consider that an emerging adult child may only partially understand the spiritual, relational, physical, and financial investment that was made to deliver them into adulthood. All that they are focused on in those early days of becoming a newly married adult is establishing their own life and family routine. So when they say no to us or resist some of our suggestions, we may become angry at them for what we perceive to be their insensitivity and ungratefulness.

If this happens, it's important that we remember that the Lord has given us knowledge that a young couple may not yet fully comprehend. We've already experienced working to preserve and enhance meaningful relationships with our own parents in the very situation that our children now find themselves.

Consider the Golden Rule: "So whatever you wish that others would do to you, do also to them" (Matthew 7:12). With that in mind, what special sensitivities can we show our child and their spouse to help smooth out the inevitable tensions that can cause division?

Responding when we feel dishonored

When we feel dishonored or sinned against by our children, the most important thing for us to do is to reflect on our own salvation and remember that although we have grieved our heavenly Father by dishonoring him with our sin, he responded to us with overflowing mercy:

> For while we were still weak, at the right time Christ died for the ungodly. For one will scarcely die for a righteous person—though perhaps for a good person one would dare even to die—but God shows his love for us in that while we were still sinners, Christ died for us. (Romans 5:6–8)

Once we've allowed that biblical framework to orient us, we can move toward forgiving our children for those ways they may have disrespected us. As C. S. Lewis says, "To be a Christian means to forgive the inexcusable, because God has forgiven the inexcusable in you."[6] Offering forgiveness in the same way Christ forgives us—perpetually, fully, and gently—goes a long way toward creating conditions in which relational turmoil can be healed. As Paul exhorts us, "Be kind to one another, tenderhearted, forgiving one another, as God in Christ forgave you" (Ephesians 4:32).

Strategies for addressing disappointment

You may understand this biblical framework but still wonder, *Is there ever a time when I should directly address dishonor I have felt from my adult child or their spouse?*

Once you have reflected on biblical passages like those noted earlier and taken time to earnestly pray and seek the counsel of your pastor or other folks in similar situations, a moment may arise when you can gently raise a concern about a circumstance in which you felt dishonored. If you feel compelled to do have such a conversation, it's best to speak with your own child first. Along the way, remember these things:

- *Create space for dialogue.* Before digging too deeply into difficult matters, develop a few questions that might draw your child out and help you to better understand the context surrounding the conflict that has occurred. You might ask, "Are you doing ok? Is there anything going on in your life that's been difficult for you that you'd like me to better understand?"

  Then give them an opportunity to express any of the ways that they may have felt disrespected by you: "Is there anything we've been doing that is making things more difficult for you? What is it that you'd like us to better understand as we move into this new phase of life?"

  By beginning with questions instead of assertions, you are creating space for dialogue and opening opportunities to learn new things about your adult children and yourselves.
- *Express your concerns gently.* If the time comes when you feel, after prayer, that you need to say something more directly, be aware of the ways that our true adversary, the devil, may try to exploit the situation to further damage the relationship with your child (Galatians 6:1).

Ask God for wisdom to express yourself in a gentle manner.

Gentleness in relational conflict sends a strong signal of care for the person you are in conflict with. You can say something like "Sometimes it feels like we aren't a part of your world at all. We know you don't mean to make us feel this way, but could we talk about how to work on it?"

- *Express your concerns constructively.* It's also helpful to have a forward-facing mindset when working through disappointment. Frame the conversation in a way that looks forward: "What can we both do better in the future to help us understand one another better?" Use the conversation that follows to develop new ideas for improving the way you relate with one another.

Conclusion

The day after our daughter's wedding, we had the privilege of taking a short vacation with our closest friends who had already married off all three of their daughters. It was a sweet time of refreshment but an even better time of listening to their stories about how the Lord not only preserved them but deepened the bond between them, their daughters, and their sons-in-law.

When we asked them what advice they had for us as we began a similar journey with our kids, they simply said, "Trust the Lord and keep making yourself available to them."

The day when our children say "I do" is a critical moment when our relationship with them changes. Such a major family transition requires us as parents to take a prayerful and thoughtful approach. There's no doubt that we will all make mistakes. But remember this: The Lord's grace is sufficient for all of us (2 Corinthians 12:9), and "his mercies . . . are new every morning" (Lamentations 3:22–23). So, in the words of one of my favorite seminary professors, "Blessed is the one who never stops starting over!"

---

1. Diana Baumrind, "Effects of Authoritative Parental Control on Child Behavior," *Child Development* 37, no. 4 (1966): 887–907, https://doi.org/10.2307/1126611.

2. Timothy Keller and Kathy Keller, *The Meaning of Marriage: Facing the Complexities of Commitment with the Wisdom of God.* (Dutton, 2011), 135.

3. For this and other stories about our lives, see my wife's blog at *KatiePolski.com.*

4. Terry & Roberts, "Facts About Divorce in America 2024," *Terry & Roberts* (blog), May 6, 2024, https://terryandrobertslaw.com/blog/divorce-rate-facts/.

5. Strong's Exhaustive Concordance, "3513. kabad or kabed," https://biblehub.com/hebrew/3513.htm.

6. C. S. Lewis, "On Forgiveness," in *The Weight of Glory and Other Addresses* (HarperOne, 2001), 181.